This Starfish Bay book belongs to

....

Go, Green Gecko!

The myriad children of Rūaumoko, the god of earthquakes, under the earth ...

To the children who take the time to stop and look

Go, Green Gecko!

Written by Gay Hay

Illustrated by Margaret Tolland

STARFISH BAY
CHILDREN'S BOOKS

The morning sun is rising.
Gecko is up and out,
basking in the treetops,
soaking up the sun.

Scuttling along branches,
snatching at flies.

*Watching out for danger,
looking all around.*

Scrambling over rata trees,
sipping sweet nectar.

Watching out for danger,
looking here and there.

Tumbling into thick ferns,
munching butterflies.

Watching out for danger,
looking in and out.

Sneaking through wet grass,
licking morning dew.

Watching out for danger,
looking near and far.

Squeezing past big boulders,
gobbling up a beetle.

Watching out for danger,
looking up and down.

Slithering over rotten logs,
gulping down a spider.

Watching out for danger,
looking round about.

Scurrying along a riverbank,
sneaking up on dragonflies.

Watching out for danger,

looking high and low.

Hanging by its long tail,
reaching out for berries.

Watching out for danger,
looking far and wide.

Scamper!
Scurry!
Hurry back ...

Down the tree,

along the riverbank,

Go, green gecko!

across the rotten logs,

past the boulders,

through the grass,

into the ferns,

over the rata trees,

along the branches.

Back in the treetops.

Safe.

Take a closer look

The gecko's skin is soft and loose and covered with tiny scales. As the gecko grows, it needs a larger skin, so it sheds its old skin. Underneath, it has a new skin that's just the right size.

Instead of eyelids that shut, the gecko has clear skin over its eyes. It licks its eyes with its special tongue to keep them clean and moist. Its tongue is shaped like a long spoon, which is also good for scooping water and nectar from plants.

The green gecko is a small reptile. Once it was common in New Zealand, but now it is not so easy to find. The green gecko is colored bright green, like a new spring leaf. It hides easily in trees and shrubs.

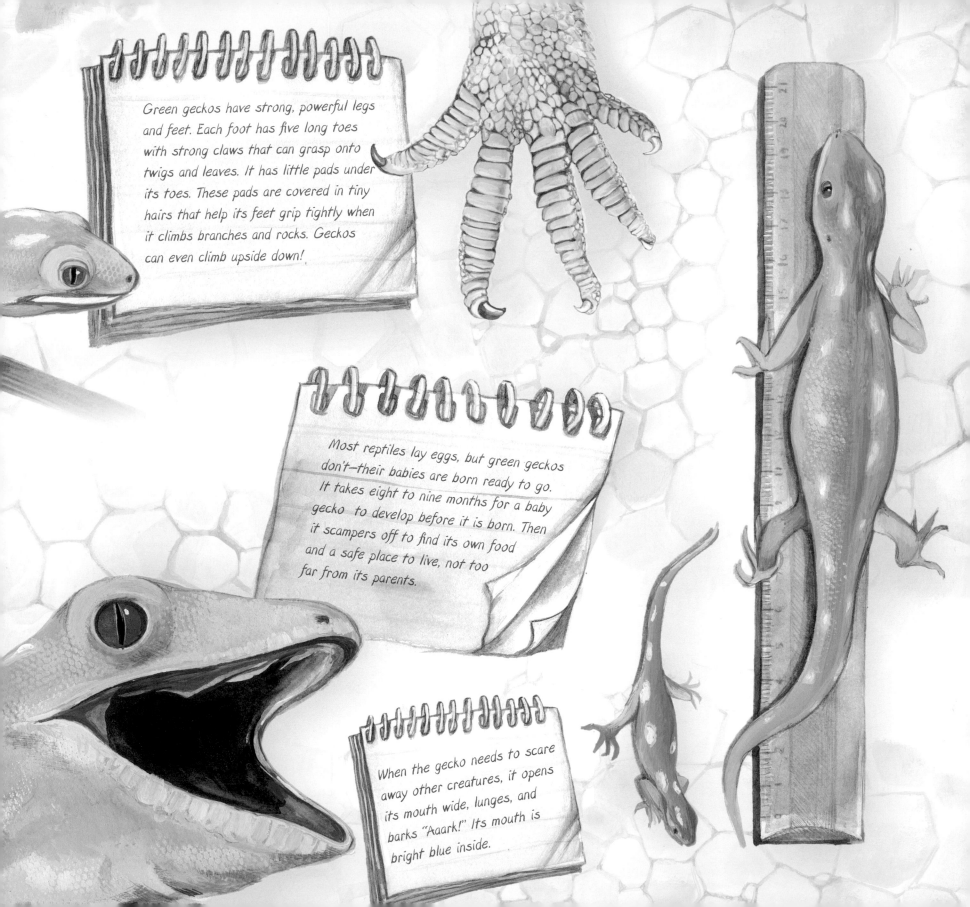

Green geckos have strong, powerful legs and feet. Each foot has five long toes with strong claws that can grasp onto twigs and leaves. It has little pads under its toes. These pads are covered in tiny hairs that help its feet grip tightly when it climbs branches and rocks. Geckos can even climb upside down!

Most reptiles lay eggs, but green geckos don't—their babies are born ready to go. It takes eight to nine months for a baby gecko to develop before it is born. Then it scampers off to find its own food and a safe place to live, not too far from its parents.

When the gecko needs to scare away other creatures, it opens its mouth wide, lunges, and barks "Aaark!" Its mouth is bright blue inside.

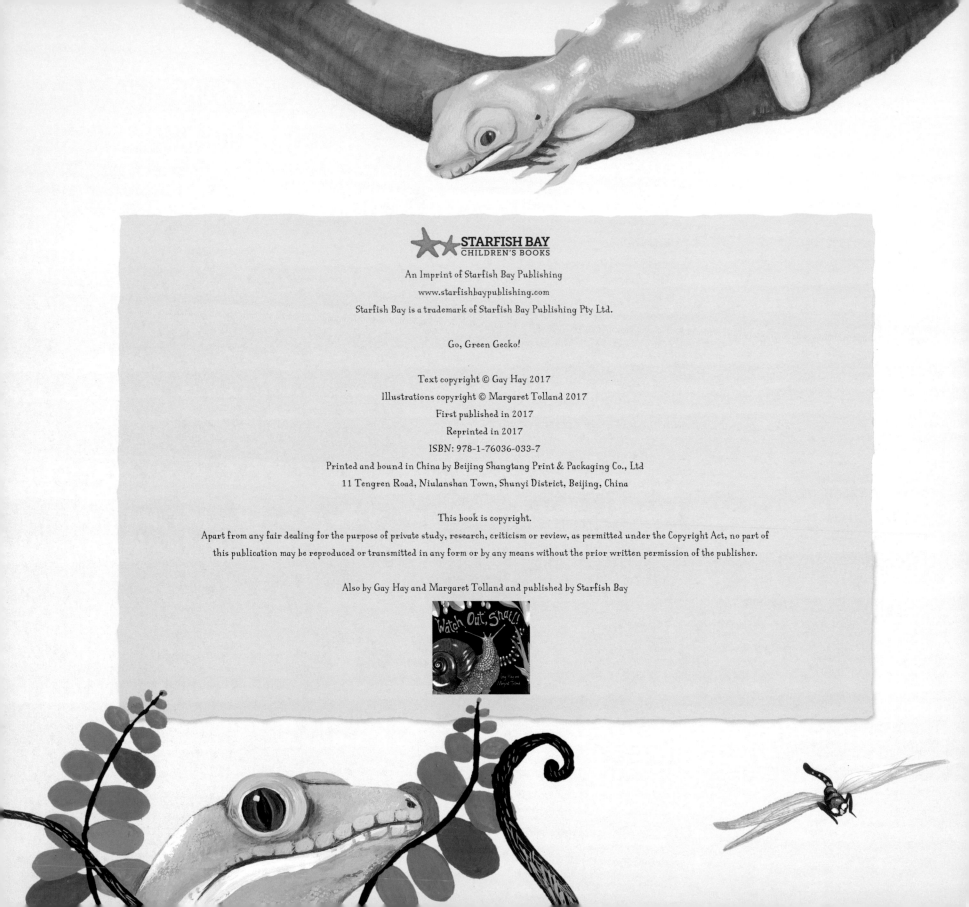

STARFISH BAY
CHILDREN'S BOOKS

An Imprint of Starfish Bay Publishing

www.starfishbaypublishing.com

Starfish Bay is a trademark of Starfish Bay Publishing Pty Ltd.

Go, Green Gecko!

First published in 2017

Reprinted in 2017

ISBN: 978-1-76036-033-7

Printed and bound in China by Beijing Shangtang Print & Packaging Co., Ltd

11 Tengren Road, Niulanshan Town, Shunyi District, Beijing, China

Also by Gay Hay and Margaret Tolland and published by Starfish Bay